PIES

Cook Books by Good Books

Phyllis Pellman Good • Rachel Thomas Pellman

Good Books

Main Street, Intercourse, PA 17534

PIES
Cook Books by Good Books

Experienced pie makers create their crusts "by feel." They know their choicest fillings by memory. We've put some tried and true favorites on paper and asked some old hands to test them.

Here, then, are family specialties for all to share. Enjoy!

Cover art and design by Cheryl A. Benner.
Design and art in body by Craig N. Heisey; Calligraphy by Gayle Smoker.
This special edition is an adaptation of *Pies: From Amish and Mennonite Kitchens, Pennsylvania Dutch Cookbooks.* Copyright © 1982, 1991 by Good Books, Intercourse, PA 17534. ISBN: 1-56148-034-7. All rights reserved. Printed in the United States of America.

Contents

Apple Pie 4
Dried Snitz Pie 5
Sour Cream Apple Pie 6
Sour Cherry Pie 7
Pumpkin Pie 8
Blueberry Pie 9
Dutch Pear Pie 10
Raisin Pie 11
Rhubarb Pie 12
Rhubarb-Strawberry Pie 13
Ground-Cherry Pie 14
Green Tomato Pie 15
Mom's Mincemeat Pie 16
Shoo Fly Pie 17
Oatmeal Pie 18
Montgomery Pie 18
Vanilla Pie 20
Grandmother Shenk's Lemon Pie 21
Lemon Sponge Pie 22
Lemon Crumb Pie 22
Old-Fashioned Baked Custard Pie 24
Coconut Custard Pie 24
Coconut Pie 25
Peanut Butter Pie 26
Pecan Pie 27
Walnut Custard Pie 28
Cheese Pie 29
Thick Milk Pie 30
Never Fail Pie Crust 31
Snails 31
Sour Cream Raspberry Pie 32

Apple Pie

6 cups apples,   Makes 1 9" pie
    peeled and sliced
¾ cup sugar
¼ cup flour
1 tsp. cinnamon
3 Tbsp. water
1 9" unbaked pie shell

1. Pour peeled and sliced apples into unbaked pie shell.
2. Combine sugar, flour, cinnamon, and water. Stir until smooth. Pour over apples.
3. Cover with top crust. Seal edges.
4. Bake at 375° for 1 hour.

Variations:

1. Stir apples into sugar, flour, and cinnamon mixture. Pour into pie shell and sprinkle with water. Cover with crumb topping made by mixing ½ cup butter or margarine, ½ cup brown sugar, and 1 cup flour.

2. Delete cinnamon. Add 1½ tsp. grated orange peel and ¼ cup quick cooking tapioca. In place of 1 cup apples use 1 cup cranberries.

3. Stir apples into sugar, flour, and cinnamon mixture. Pour into pie shell and sprinkle with water. Cover with coconut streusel topping made by mixing ⅓ cup brown sugar, ⅓ cup graham cracker crumbs, ¼ cup softened butter, and ½ cup flaked coconut.

Dried Snitz Pie

3 cups dried apples   Makes 1 9" pie
2¼ cups warm water
1 tsp. lemon extract
⅔ cup brown sugar
1 double crust 9" unbaked pie shell

1. Soak apples in the warm water. Cook over low heat until soft.
2. Mash apples and add lemon and sugar.
3. Pour into unbaked pie shell. Cover with top crust. Seal edges.
4. Bake at 425° for 15 minutes; then at 350° for 30 minutes. Serve warm.

Sour Cream Apple Pie

Makes 1 9" pie

2 Tbsp. flour
½ cup sugar
¼ tsp salt
2½ cups chopped, pared apples
1 cup sour cream
1 egg
1½ tsp. vanilla
1 9" unbaked pie shell

1. Combine flour, sugar, and salt. Mix with apples. Pour into unbaked pie shell.
2. Beat together sour cream, egg, and vanilla. Pour over apple mixture.
3. Bake at 425° for 15 minutes and then at 350° for 30 minutes. Remove from oven and sprinkle with crumb mixture. Bake 10 minutes more at 400°.

Crumbs:

⅓ cup flour
⅓ cup sugar
1½ tsp. cinnamon
¼ cup butter

Combine all ingredients and mix to form fine crumbs.

Sour Cherry Pie

1¼ cups cherry juice   Makes 1 9" pie
1½ cups water
⅛ tsp. salt
¾ cup sugar
5½ Tbsp. tapioca
¼ tsp. almond extract
3 cups canned sour cherries, drained
1 9" unbaked pie shell

1. Heat cherry juice and 1 cup water.
2. Mix tapioca, sugar, and salt with ½ cup water until smooth. Stir slowly into hot juice and water, stirring and cooking until thickened.
3. Add almond extract. Remove from heat. Add cherries. Chill until cold. Pour into unbaked 9" pie shell. Top with pastry strips to form lattice or bake without and top with crumbs when pie is partly finished.
4. Bake at 400° on lowest oven shelf for 10-15 minutes; then turn oven to 350° and bake until finished (lower heat if pie gets too brown).

Variation:
Substitute 2 rounded Tbsp. of strawberry Danish Dessert and 3½ Tbsp. clear-jell for 5½ Tbsp. tapioca.

Pumpkin Pie

1½ cup mashed pumpkin   Makes 1 9" pie
   or butternut squash
1 egg
½ cup milk, heated
½ cup cream, heated
1 Tbsp. flour
1 Tbsp. molasses or King Syrup
¾ cup sugar
1 tsp. cinnamon
dash of nutmeg
1 Tbsp. browned butter
pinch of salt
1 9" unbaked pie shell

1. Combine all ingredients. Pour into unbaked pie shell. Sprinkle additional cinnamon and nutmeg over top of pie.

2. Bake at 450° for 15 minutes; then at 350° for 45 minutes.

Variation:
   Add ½ cup coconut to pie mixture or sprinkle coconut in bottom of pie shell before filling, or on top of filled pie before baking.

Blueberry Pie

2¾ cups blueberries   Makes 1 9" pie
juice from berries plus water to make
   ½ cup liquid
½ cup sugar
3 Tbsp. tapioca
1 9" unbaked pie crust

1. Combine blueberries, liquid, sugar, and tapioca. Toss lightly to mix.
2. Pour into unbaked pie shell. Cover with crumbs or pastry. Bake at 400° for 10 minutes; then at 350° for 30 minutes.

Dutch Pear Pie

¼ cup flour   Makes 1 9" pie
¾ cup sugar
1 cup cream or canned evaporated milk
1 Tbsp. lemon juice
5 fresh pears, peeled and diced or canned
    pears in light syrup
¼ tsp. cinnamon
1 Tbsp. sugar
1 9" unbaked pie shell

1. Sift together flour and sugar. Stir in cream
and lemon juice. Mix until smooth. Add
pears. Pour into an unbaked pie shell.
Sprinkle top with sugar and cinnamon.
2. Bake at 400° for 45-50 minutes. Cool
until set.

    Apples or peaches may be used instead
of pears for an equally tasty pie.

Raisin Pie

2 cups raisins   Makes 1 9" pie
2 cups cold water
1½ cups sugar
4 Tbsp. flour
2 eggs, separated
¼ tsp. salt
4 Tbsp. melted butter
1 Tbsp. vinegar or lemon juice
1 9" baked pie shell

1. In saucepan combine raisins, 1½ cups water and 1 cup sugar and bring to a boil. Combine the remaining ½ cup water and ½ cup sugar, plus flour, egg yolks, and salt; add to raisin mixture. Cook until thickened, stirring constantly. Remove from heat and add butter and vinegar or lemon juice.

2. Pour mixture into baked pie shell. Cover with whipped cream or meringue.

Meringue:

Beat egg whites till stiff peaks form. Gradually add 2 Tbsp. sugar while beating. Pile on top of pie and bake at 350° till golden brown, about 10 minutes.

Rhubarb Pie

3 cups diced rhubarb   Makes 1 9" pie
1¼ cups sugar
¼ tsp. salt
2 Tbsp. water
3 Tbsp. flour
1 Tbsp. lemon juice
2 eggs
1 9" unbaked pie shell

1. Place rhubarb in unbaked pie shell.
2. Combine remaining ingredients and stir
to form a smooth paste.
3. Cover with crumbs made by mixing 3 Tbsp.
flour, 3 Tbsp. sugar, and 2 Tbsp. butter.
4. Bake at 425° for 10 minutes; then at
325° for 30 more minutes.

Variation:
    Separate eggs and add only yolks to paste
mixture. Beat whites with 2 Tbsp. sugar
and ¼ tsp. cream of tartar until stiff peaks
form. Instead of crumb topping, pile meringue
on pie during last few minutes of baking time.
Bake meringue until lightly browned.

Rhubarb-Strawberry Pie

1 pt. fresh strawberries   Makes 1 9" pie
2 cups sliced raw rhubarb
¾ cup brown sugar
½ cup sugar
1 tsp. grated lemon rind
1 double crust 9" unbaked pie shell

1. Slice strawberries and rhubarb.
2. Combine sugars and lemon rind and toss lightly with fruit. Pour into pie shell. Cover with top crust. Seal edges.
3. Bake at 350° for 50 minutes.

"Tangy and delicious!"

Ground-Cherry Pie

2½ cups ground-cherries   Makes 1 8" pie
½ cup brown sugar
1 Tbsp. flour
1 Tbsp. minute tapioca
3 Tbsp. water
2 Tbsp. butter or margarine
1 two-crust unbaked 8" pie shell

1. Wash ground-cherries and place in unbaked pie shell. Mix sugar, flour, and tapioca and sprinkle over cherries. Dribble water over top. Dot with butter or margarine.
2. Cover with top crust. Seal edges.
3. Bake 15 minutes at 400°; reduce temperature to 375° and bake 30 minutes longer.

Ground-cherries are a fruit distinct from the more common sweet cherries and sour cherries. They grow on low bushes; each cherry is encased in a paper-like pod.

Green Tomato Pie

Makes 1 10" pie

4 cups tomatoes
1 cup brown sugar
1 tsp. cinnamon
½ tsp. cloves
1 double crust 10" unbaked pie shell

1. Wash tomatoes but do not pare. Slice in thin rings ½ hour before using. After draining for ½ hour, pour away juice.
2. Combine tomatoes, sugar, and spices.
3. Sprinkle bottom of pie crust with flour. Pour in tomato mixture. Sprinkle with flour. Cover with top crust. Seal edges.
4. Bake at 425° for 15 minutes; then at 375° for 30 minutes.

"It's spicy and delicious! My family keeps asking for it."

Mom's Mincemeat Pie

2 cups cooked beef, ground   Makes 1 9" pie
3 cups raw apples, ground
½ cup brown sugar
¼ tsp. salt
1 tsp. cinnamon
½ tsp. cloves (optional)
2 Tbsp. whiskey
4 Tbsp. Black Cherry wine
raisins (optional)
1 double crust 9" unbaked pie shell

1. Combine beef, apples, sugar, salt, and spices in saucepan. Cook over low heat till thoroughly heated. (Add beef broth if needed to keep from getting dry.)
2. Stir in whiskey, wine, and raisins.
3. Pour into unbaked pie shell. Cover with top crust. Seal edges.
4. Bake at 350° for 45 minutes. Serve hot.

"Mom's mincemeat pie is the best mincemeat pie I've ever tasted."

Variation:
Mincemeat may be frozen after step #1. To use, thaw and stir in whiskey, wine, and raisins.

Shoo Fly Pie

Crumbs:

1 cup flour
1 Tbsp. shortening
⅔ cup light brown sugar

Cut together with 2 knives till crumbly. Take out ½ cup crumbs and set aside.

Bottom Part:
1 egg slightly beaten
1 cup molasses
1 cup boiling water
1 tsp. baking soda
1 9" unbaked pie shell

1. To crumb mixture add egg and molasses. Add ¾ cup boiling water. Dissolve soda in remaining ¼ cup water and add last.
2. Pour into unbaked pie shell. Sprinkle reserved crumbs on top. Bake at 425° for 15 minutes. Reduce heat to 350° and bake 40-45 minutes longer.

Oatmeal Pie

4 eggs, slightly beaten   Makes 2 8" pies
1 cup sugar
1½ cups molasses
1 cup milk
1½ cups oatmeal
1 Tbsp. melted butter
¼ tsp. salt
2 tsp. vanilla
½ cup chopped nuts
2 8" unbaked pie shells

1. Combine all ingredients. Pour into 2 unbaked pie shells.
2. Bake at 350° for 40-45 minutes.

Montgomery Pie

Syrup: Makes 4 8" pies
juice and grated rind of 1 lemon
1 cup molasses
1 pt. water
1 cup sugar
1 Tbsp. flour
1 egg

Combine all ingredients and mix well. Divide syrup among 4 unbaked pie shells.

Top Part:
- ½ cup shortening
- 2 cups sugar
- 2 eggs
- 1 cup milk
- 2½ cups flour
- 2½ tsp. baking powder

1. Cream shortening and sugar. Add eggs and beat well.
2. Add milk alternately with flour and baking powder.
3. Divide batter and pour over the syrup in the 4 unbaked pie shells. Bake at 450° for 15 minutes; then at 350° for 45 minutes.

"This is an old family recipe from Grandma Neff's collection."

Vanilla Pie

Bottom Part: Makes 2 9" pies

   1 cup sugar
   1 cup molasses
   2 cups water
   1 egg, well beaten
   3 Tbsp. flour
   1 tsp. vanilla
   2 9" unbaked pie shells

1. In saucepan, combine all ingredients except vanilla. Boil until thick. Set aside to cool. When cooled, stir in vanilla. Pour into unbaked pie shells.

Crumbs:

   2 cups flour
   ¾ cup sugar
   ½ cup butter or margarine
   1 tsp. cream of tartar
   1 tsp. soda

1. Mix all ingredients together to form crumbs. Sprinkle over tops of pies.
2. Bake at 375° for 50-60 minutes.

Grandmother Shenk's Lemon Pie

Makes 2 8" pies

1 cup sugar
1/4 cup butter
2 eggs
1/2 cup flour
1 tsp. soda
2 cups water
Juice and grated rind of 1 lemon
2 8" unbaked pie shells

1. Cream sugar and butter. Add eggs and beat well. Add flour and soda and beat. Add water, lemon juice and grated rind and mix.

2. Pour into 2 unbaked pie shells. Bake at 425° for 15 minutes then reduce temperature to 350° and continue baking for 25-30 minutes.

"A quick and easy recipe that tastes good."

Lemon Sponge Pie

Makes 1 9" pie

1 cup sugar
2 Tbsp. butter
3 eggs, separated
3 Tbsp. flour
½ tsp. salt
Juice and grated rind of 1 lemon
1½ cups hot water or milk
1 9" unbaked pie shell

1. Cream sugar and butter. Add egg yolks and beat well. Add flour, salt, lemon juice and rind. Add water or milk. Fold in stiffly beaten egg whites.
2. Pour into unbaked pie shell. Bake at 325° for 45-50 minutes.

Lemon Crumb Pie

Bottom Part:

Makes 2 9" pies

½ cup shortening
1 cup sugar
1 tsp. baking soda
3½ cups flour
¾ cup sour milk

22

1. Cream shortening and sugar. Add baking soda. Add flour alternately with sour milk. Batter will be stiff and sticky.
2. Roll dough ¼" thick and press into pie pans. Reserve enough dough for thin strips on top of filling.

Filling:

   1 cup sugar
   juice and grated rind of 1 lemon
   ½ cup molasses
   2 Tbsp. cornstarch
   1 cup water

1. Combine sugar, lemon, and molasses in a saucepan. Bring to a boil.
2. Combine cornstarch and water and stir till smooth. Gradually add to boiling mixture, stirring constantly. Cook till clear and slightly thickened.
3. Pour into dough-lined pie pans. Cover with strips of dough.
4. Bake at 350° for 25-30 minutes.

Old-Fashioned Baked Custard Pie

⅓ cup sugar   Makes 1 9" pie
2 tsp. flour
½ tsp. salt
3 eggs
3 cups milk
¼ tsp. nutmeg
1 9" unbaked pie shell

1. Combine sugar, flour, and salt with eggs and mix until smooth.
2. Heat milk to boiling point. And 1 cup hot milk to egg mixture and then pour into remaining hot milk.
3. Pour into unbaked pie shell. Sprinkle nutmeg over top. Bake at 350° for 40-45 minutes.

Coconut Custard Pie

2⅔ cups milk   Makes 1 9" pie
½ cup sugar
½ tsp. salt
1 tsp. vanilla
4 eggs
½ cup grated coconut
1 9" unbaked pie shell

1. Combine milk, sugar, salt, and vanilla in saucepan. Heat to scalding.

2. Beat eggs lightly. Slowly add scalded ingredients to beaten eggs.

3. Pour into unbaked pie shell. Sprinkle coconut over top of filling. Bake at 450° for 10 minutes and then at 350° for 15-20 minutes or until set.

Coconut Pie

½ cup brown sugar   Makes 1 9" pie
¼ cup flour
½ cup coconut
¼ tsp. soda
½ cup molasses
¼ cup sour cream
¾ cup milk
1 egg, beaten
1 9" unbaked pie shell

1. Combine sugar, flour, coconut, and soda. Add molasses, sour cream, milk, and beaten egg. Mix well.

2. Pour into unbaked pie shell. Bake at 350° for 10 minutes and then at 325° for 35-40 minutes.

Peanut Butter Pie

Crumbs:
Makes 1 9" pie

2/3 cup 10x sugar
1/3 cup crunchy peanut butter

1. Mix together until fine crumbs are formed. Sprinkle 1/2 of crumb mixture in bottom of baked pie shell. Reserve other half of crumbs for topping.

Filling:

2 egg yolks, beaten
1/3 cup sugar
1 Tbsp. flour
1 Tbsp. cornstarch
2 cups milk
1 Tbsp. butter
1 tsp. vanilla
1 9" baked pie shell

1. Combine sugar, flour, and cornstarch. Add to beaten egg yolks. Mix to form a smooth paste. Add milk and cook, stirring constantly until thickened. Remove from heat and stir in butter and vanilla.

2. Pour partly cooled filling into baked pie shell. When cooled sprinkle with remaining crumb mixture. Serve with whipped cream.

Pecan Pie

2 Tbsp. butter   Makes 1 8" pie
¼ cup sugar
2 eggs
¾ cup molasses
1 Tbsp. flour
1 tsp. vanilla
pinch salt
¾ cup water
½ cup pecans
1 8" unbaked pie shell

1. Cream butter, sugar, and eggs. Add molasses, flour, vanilla, and salt.
2. Stir in water and pecans.
3. Pour into unbaked pie shell.
4. Bake at 450° for 10 minutes; then at 350° for 25-30 minutes.

Walnut Custard Pie

3 Tbsp. flour   Makes 2 8" pies
½ cup water
1 cup sugar
2 eggs, beaten
¾ cup King Syrup molasses
1½ cups milk
1½ cups walnuts
2 8" baked pie shells

1. Combine flour and water and stir to make a smooth paste. Add sugar, eggs, molasses, and milk.
2. Cook over medium high heat until thickened, stirring constantly.
3. Cool. Add walnuts. Pour into baked pie shells. Allow to stand for several hours before cutting.

"Rich ... and chewy."

Cheese Pie

1 - 8 oz. pkg. cream cheese   Makes 1 10" pie
2 eggs, separated
¾ cup sugar
2 Tbsp. flour
dash of salt
½ tsp. vanilla
1 cup evaporated milk
1 cup sweet milk
1 10" unbaked pie shell

1. Soften cream cheese. In mixing bowl combine cheese, egg yolks, sugar, flour, salt, and vanilla. Beat until smooth.
2. Add evaporated milk a bit at a time and beat till smooth. Gradually add remaining milk.
3. Fold in stiffly beaten egg whites.
4. Pour into chilled, unbaked pie shell. Bake for 15 minutes at 400°; then 15 minutes at 375°; then 15 minutes at 325°.

"This is delicious served with molasses."

Thick Milk Pie

3 eggs

Makes 2   9" pies

1 cup molasses
1 cup sugar
½ cup flour
1 tsp. soda
3 cups thick, sour milk
2 9" unbaked pie shells

1. Beat eggs. Add molasses.
2. Combine sugar, flour, and soda and add to egg mixture. Add thick milk. Pour into 2 unbaked pie shells.
3. Bake at 400° for 10 minutes; then at 325° for 40-45 minutes.

Variation:
   Sprinkle top of pie with cinnamon.

"Yummy... delicious! Tastes like pumpkin, coconut, and shoo fly pie!"

Never Fail Pie Crust

3 cups flour   Makes 4 9" pie shells
1 tsp. salt
1¼ cup vegetable shortening
1 egg, beaten
⅓ cup cold water
1 Tbsp. vinegar

1. Mix flour and salt. Cut in shortening.
2. Combine remaining ingredients and stir into shortening mixture. Let stand a few minutes.
3. Roll dough on floured board to desired thickness.

Snails

1. Use left over pie dough. Roll out, spread with butter, brown sugar, and cinnamon.
2. Roll up like a jelly roll, slice and bake at 375° for 12 minutes or until brown.

Sour Cream Raspberry Pie

2 Tbsp. flour   Makes 1 9" pie
1 qt. raspberries
1 cup sour cream
2-3 Tbsp. sugar
1 9" unbaked pie shell

1. Sprinkle flour on bottom of unbaked pie shell. Fill with the raspberries. Spread sour cream over top of berries. Sprinkle with sugar.
2. Bake at 375° for 30-40 minutes until golden and bubbly.

The Little Mermaid

Retold by Justine Korman • Illustrated by Cristina Ong

Cartwheel
·B·O·O·K·S·™

SCHOLASTIC INC.

New York   Toronto   London   Auckland   Sydney

Text copyright © 1993 by Scholastic Inc.
Illustrations copyright © 1993 by Cristina Ong.
All rights reserved. Published by Scholastic Inc.
CARTWHEEL BOOKS™ is a trademark of Scholastic Inc.

ISBN 0-590-46448-5

12 11 10 9 8 7 6 5 4 3 2 1   3 4 5 6 7 8/9
Printed in the U.S.A.   24
First Scholastic printing, August 1993

Once upon a time at the bottom of the sea, there lived the King of the Mermaids and his six lovely daughters. The mermaids spent their days tending the gardens around the Mer-king's splendid castle, playing with pretty fishes, and singing.

Everyone praised the youngest mermaid's beautiful voice. But all the Little Mermaid dreamed of was life above the rolling waves.

The Little Mermaid loved her grandmother's stories of the world above. She told of ships and land, cities and people, and birds who sang and flew through the sky. The Little Mermaid longed to see these wonders for herself. But she would have to wait until she was fifteen years old.

Finally the great day arrived. The Little Mermaid rose like a bubble to the surface of the sea. She marveled at the glorious sunset. Then she swam toward the sound of music coming from a great sailing ship.

Everyone on the ship made merry to celebrate
the prince's sixteenth birthday. Sailors danced and
fireworks exploded in the evening sky.

At first, the Little Mermaid feared the showers of
rainbow sparks. Then, she enjoyed their beauty. But
she thought the most wonderful sight of all was the
smiling young prince.

As the fireworks grew silent, the ocean started to rumble. Suddenly the prince's ship was tossed by a terrible storm. The ship began to sink.

The Little Mermaid quickly realized that the handsome prince would drown! She dove through the dark and angry waves until she found him. Then the Little Mermaid held the prince's head above the churning water.

As morning dawned, the sea finally
calmed. The Little Mermaid tenderly carried
the prince to shore. She kissed him and left
him safe on the warm sand.

The Little Mermaid swam behind some
rocks and waited to see who would find
the prince.

A young girl strolling the beach came upon the handsome prince. She bent over him. The prince's dark eyes fluttered open. He smiled at the girl he thought had saved him.

The Little Mermaid turned away and dove sadly into the depths of the sea.

The Little Mermaid could not forget her prince. Every day she rose to the surface of the water and searched for him. She fell deeper and deeper in love.

"I wish I were human," she told her grandmother.

"Don't be foolish," the old mermaid said. "We swim the oceans for 300 years. Then we turn into sea foam. Humans have a much shorter time. But when their lives end, good people rise to heaven and live forever."

"I want to go to heaven, too," the Little Mermaid said.

"Only humans can go to heaven," her grandmother said. "And to become human, you would need legs instead of your pretty fish tail."

Desperate to win the prince's love, the Little Mermaid swam to the horrible sea witch.

"I can mix a potion that will turn your tail into pretty legs," cackled the witch, "but each time your feet touch the ground it will feel as if you are walking on knives. And if the prince falls in love with another, on the morning after his marriage you will turn into foam on the ocean."

The Little Mermaid swallowed hard. "I still want to try," she said.

The sea witch's evil eyes glowed with greed. "First, you must pay for the potion. You must give me your beautiful voice."

Because the Little Mermaid loved the prince so much, she agreed. Immediately, she fell silent. She could no longer sing or speak.

The next day at dawn, the Little Mermaid
went to the steps of the prince's castle. She
drank the precious potion, and felt as if
a sword were cutting her in two.
The Little Mermaid fainted.

When she awoke, the prince was standing over her. And where her fish tail had been, were two lovely, slender legs.

The prince asked the Little Mermaid who she was and where she had come from. But she had no voice to answer with. The Little Mermaid could only look at him with eyes as deep and blue as the ocean.

The prince helped the Little Mermaid up to his castle. Though each step felt like knives stabbing her feet, she was glad to walk at his side.

Soon she was dressed in royal silks and presented to the court. Everyone thought the Little Mermaid was lovely, even though she could not speak.

Since she was unable to charm the prince with her beautiful singing, the Little Mermaid danced. Each step was torture. But when she saw the prince's smile, she did not mind the pain.

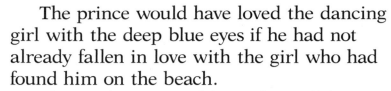

The prince would have loved the dancing
girl with the deep blue eyes if he had not
already fallen in love with the girl who had
found him on the beach.

The Little Mermaid longed to tell him
she was really the one who had saved him.
But she could not say a word.

When the king and queen decided the prince must marry, they arranged for him to sail to the next kingdom to meet a beautiful princess. To the prince's amazement and delight, the princess was the girl who he thought had rescued him!

Soon the happy couple was married. The Little Mermaid held up the long train of the bride's dress as she walked down the aisle. But she did not hear the ceremony or the music. She did not listen to the good wishes of the happy crowd. For the Little Mermaid's heart was breaking. And she knew the next morning she would be nothing but foam on the sea.

During the celebration aboard the prince's ship, the Little Mermaid danced more gracefully than ever. The pain in her feet was nothing compared to the ache in her heart.

That night, the Little Mermaid sat alone on the deck. Tears fell from her eyes as she stared sadly out to sea. Then her sisters bobbed to the surface. Their heads looked strangely small without their long, flowing hair.

"We gave our hair to the sea witch to save you," the Little Mermaid's sisters explained. Then the oldest handed her a magic knife. "If you stab the prince," she said, "you may return to the sea. You will live as a mermaid once again."

The Little Mermaid went to the room
where the prince and his bride slept. The
knife trembled in her hand as she gazed
upon the prince. Although he loved another,
the Little Mermaid could not kill him. Not
even to save her own life.

The Little Mermaid ran to the sea and
tossed the knife into the waves. She watched
as its evil magic bubbled away. Then, as the
first rays of dawn sparkled over the water,
she dived in. The Little Mermaid felt as if
she were dissolving into foam.

But she did not die. Instead of turning
into foam, the Little Mermaid floated up
into the light. She heard beautiful singing.
Suddenly she could sing, too!

Because the Little Mermaid had spared
the prince, she had become one of the air
spirits who fly around the world doing good
deeds. And her spirit lives still, bringing joy
to people everywhere whenever she smiles
down upon them.

She also lives right here on Earth, as a story grandmothers tell their children about the brave Little Mermaid whose heart was full of love.